MOODS OF THE
SOUTH HAMS

PETER WHITE

HALSGROVE

First published in Great Britain in 2004

British Library Cataloguing-in-Publication Data
A CIP record for this title is available from the British Library

ISBN 1 84114 387 1

HALSGROVE
Halsgrove House
Lower Moor Way
Tiverton, Devon EX16 6SS
Tel: 01884 243242
Fax: 01884 243325
email: sales@halsgrove.com
website: www.halsgrove.com

Printed and bound by D'Auria Industrie Grafiche Spa, Italy

Calm anchorage at the mouth of the Yealm.

CONTENTS

INTRODUCTION
The South Hams – a very special part of Devon

My first experience of the South Hams was on a cycling trip around the West Country when I was quite young. We stayed for a couple of nights at Maypool Youth Hostel, perched high above the Dart Estuary looking down to Dartmouth and Kingswear. Coming from London, I had never seen that sort of landscape before, and I thought it was wonderful. Wild coast and lonely estuaries, busy harbours and ancient towns, all with a green hinterland of rolling hills and steep wooded valleys rising up to the distant heights of Dartmoor. This was English landscape at its best.

Ten years later, in 1967, I returned to Devon to take up my first ever job. I found it difficult to believe that I was actually being paid to work here, and I used every spare moment to explore. The South Hams took a lot of my time. It is one of those landscapes which grows on you – the better you get to know it, the more it has to offer. Wonderful places and magical moments linger in the memory: the day I discovered Westcombe Beach, rough seas battling the tide race off Start Point, surfing glassy swells at Bantham, swimming in crystal-clear water at Elender Cove, exploring the Avon Estuary in my canoe, watching the sun set over Bigbury Bay.

Since those early days I have travelled over much of Europe and further afield, but I still rank the South Hams, and in particular its coastline, as one of my favourite places. I count myself lucky to live so close to it, and even luckier to have the opportunity to put together this photographic study of the area. I can think of nowhere else with such a pleasing combination of landscapes, which somehow combine into one harmonious whole. The main river valleys – Dart, Avon, Erme, and Yealm – are perhaps the key to this harmony, providing the links between areas of very different character. High up on Dartmoor they cut wild and rocky valleys before winding through softer countryside and then becoming those wonderful tidal estuaries which meet the open sea in such dramatic and beautiful locations. The coastline between them is rugged and wild over much of its length, but you will find remote sandy coves, busy holiday beaches, little fishing villages, carpets of wild flowers, days of sunshine and calm, and other days of thundering surf, spume and spray. Even the towns around the coast and up the estuaries seem to be a part of the landscape rather than an imposition upon it. They grow out of the water and climb prettily up the slopes above. The whole seems to have a logic, to be a microcosm of what England is, or perhaps what it should be.

My approach to photography is simplistic. The most important bits of my kit are a map, tide tables, walking boots, the weather forecast and a willingness to spend time getting to know and understand the character and moods of the landscape. My camera is an ancient Olympus OM1 with a few lenses and filters – good quality, but very low-tech! Nothing gets tweaked on the computer. Nature is beautiful enough without me trying to improve upon it, and I get my satisfaction from knowing where and when to find that beauty, and how to capture it on film.

My thanks go to Halsgrove for giving me the opportunity to put this second book together; and to my wife, Linda, who has provided foreground interest where necessary, shaded lenses, waited patiently for the sun to come out or go in, and yet has offered encouragement and constructive criticism throughout! With her help I have managed to produce something which I am pleased with, which I believe does justice to a very special part of this country, and which I hope will be enjoyed by you, the reader. In the next few pages you will find a selection of shots giving a flavour of the whole area, followed by six chapters which take us on a journey around the coast from Torbay to Plymouth and then inland and up on to Dartmoor.

Sunset at Hope Cove.

THE SOUTH HAMS

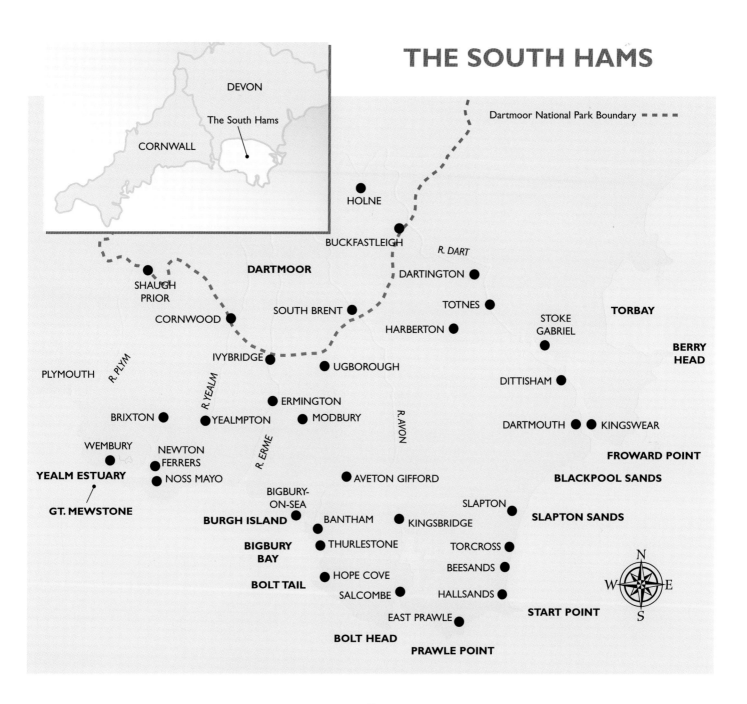

DEVON

The South Hams

CORNWALL

Dartmoor National Park Boundary

HOLNE

BUCKFASTLEIGH

R. DART

DARTINGTON

DARTMOOR

SHAUGH PRIOR

SOUTH BRENT

TOTNES

TORBAY

CORNWOOD

HARBERTON

STOKE GABRIEL

BERRY HEAD

IVYBRIDGE

UGBOROUGH

PLYMOUTH

R. PLYM

DITTISHAM

R. YEALM

ERMINGTON

BRIXTON

YEALMPTON

MODBURY

R. AVON

DARTMOUTH

KINGSWEAR

WEMBURY

NEWTON FERRERS

R. ERME

FROWARD POINT

YEALM ESTUARY

NOSS MAYO

AVETON GIFFORD

BLACKPOOL SANDS

GT. MEWSTONE

BIGBURY-ON-SEA

SLAPTON

SLAPTON SANDS

BURGH ISLAND

BANTHAM

KINGSBRIDGE

BIGBURY BAY

THURLESTONE

TORCROSS

BEESANDS

HOPE COVE

BOLT TAIL

SALCOMBE

HALLSANDS

START POINT

EAST PRAWLE

BOLT HEAD

PRAWLE POINT

N
W E
S

Salcombe and the beaches of East Portlemouth from Sharp Tor – a view which sums up the South Hams landscape.

Wonwell Beach, a good spot for surf.

Westcombe Beach with its wonderful rock architecture.

The Great Mew Stone – a notable landmark offshore from Wembury.

Impressive cliffs and stacks west of Ayrmer Cove.

One of the dramatic pinnacles at Sharp Tor, near Salcombe.

Clockwise from above: *Thrift or Sea Pink; Pennywort;*
Sea Campion.

Surf's up! Junior life guards in training at Bantham.

The Mew Stone off Froward Point, on a stormy day.

Peace and quiet at low tide on the Avon.

18

Busy times on the beach at Bigbury.

Dartmouth – an historic town with strong maritime traditions.

Dittisham – a beautiful village on the Dart.

Rolling farmland lapping up against Ugborough Beacon.

Hangershell Rock, looking up the Erme valley into the remoteness of Dartmoor.

Setting sail at dawn on the Dart.

TORBAY TO START POINT AND UP THE DART

From Brixham down to Start Point the coast faces south and east and is sheltered from the Atlantic swells. That is not to say that the sea is never rough – the inhabitants of Hallsands who were evacuated just before most of the village was destroyed by a great storm in 1917 would testify to that – but most of the time it is gentle and friendly.

As we leave Torbay and head south the change from holiday resort to the different delights of an undeveloped coast is rapid. The delightful little beaches at Man Sands and Scabbacombe have a lonely feel about them which makes it hard to believe that 100 000 people live just over the hill. Sit on Froward Point looking out to the dramatic rocky islet of the Mew Stone and you will feel close to nature. Seals bask on the offshore rocks at low tide, peregrine falcons patrol the cliffs and gannets dive out to sea. I once witnessed a pod of about 15 dolphins close inshore and heading east at a rate of knots – a fantastic sight which seemed to suit the place.

From here the coast turns in to the mouth of the Dart Estuary, guarded by the twin castles of Dartmouth and Kingswear. The Dart is the biggest and busiest of the South Hams estuaries. At its mouth Dartmouth, with its naval traditions and deep-water harbour, is a fascinating place. From its historic centre a labyrinth of steps and alleyways climbs up the hill to wonderful viewpoints above the town. Take a cruise on one of the many pleasure boats that ply the estuary. Glide past incredibly steep woods and fields, past grand houses and pretty little villages to historic Totnes – a beautiful mediaeval town, complete with castle, a distinctive and thriving culture all of its own, and a bustling shopping centre.

Back in Dartmouth, take the ferry down to the castle, beyond which is a series of pretty little rocky coves. Then, unfortunately, the coast path turns inland and does not regain the shore until we get beyond the village of Strete. The one beach which is accessible on this stretch is Blackpool Sands, and very pretty it is too with everything you need for a day out with the family. Further south Slapton Sands are a feature unique in Devon. The long curved shingle ridge has dammed a number of small streams to form Slapton Ley – the largest natural body of fresh water in the county, and a haven for wildlife. Torcross, at its southern end, faces the waves bravely behind sea defences completed in 1980 after severe flooding and damage. Southwards again, Beesands too looks precariously located, and at Hallsands the power of the sea is clear when you look down on what is left of the lower part of the village.

As you walk on and up towards the rocky ridge of Start Point look back at the great sweep of the coast behind you – a magnificent sight, and very different from what awaits you just around the corner beyond the lighthouse.

Man Sands – just over the hill from Torbay.

Designs on the beach.

Opposite page: *East from Outer Froward Point.*

The Mew Stone, beyond Outer Froward Point.

The daymark at the mouth of the Dart, built by the Harbour Commissioners in 1864.

Covering the mouth of the Dart.

*Dartmouth and Kingswear Castles, guarding the
harbour entrance.*

Dartmouth is busy, fascinating, and steeped in maritime history.

Dittisham at dawn.

The middle reaches of the Dart Estuary are beautiful.

Totnes is historic and colourful, and was once a thriving commercial port.

Torcross faces the sea bravely.

Blackpool Sands are popular and pretty.

Slapton Sands and Slapton Ley – unique in Devon.

A gleam of sunshine on what is left of Hallsands village.

The remains of Hallsands take a battering from the sea.

The lighthouse at Start Point.

START POINT TO BOLT TAIL VIA KINGSBRIDGE

Lighthouses have an appeal which is both aesthetic and emotional. They are functional, but beautiful, buildings at the extremities of the land, neatly symbolising our stormy relationship with the sea. The one at Start Point is no exception, marking the turn from the relative shelter of Lyme Bay into the wild Atlantic. Immediately the feel of the coast changes – the ocean is restless, the cliffs are more jagged, there are no trees. The sea is in charge here, and the coast is dramatic. But it is pretty too.

For much of the way to Prawle Point the path follows what is in fact a raised beach, uplifted in geological time and now forming a narrow bench of fertile land, running beneath the great rocky ridges of the former cliff line. Little coves offer the chance of a swim and Lannacombe Beach is good for surf. Prawle Point is the southernmost extremity of Devon, beloved of birdwatchers seeking seasonal migrants and the occasional rarity blown off course by a gale. The old Coastguard lookout on this high and rocky headland is now manned by Coastwatch volunteers and the view both ways along the coast is tremendous. The next headland to the west is the great ridge of Gammon Head, and en route there is a surprise. Amongst all this grandeur you will look down on to a perfect little beach – Elender Cove. It is difficult to imagine anywhere more idyllic. But tear yourself away and press on to East Portlemouth. This is exhilarating walking, high up on the cliffs above a series of remote beaches and then, as you round the corner, the town of Salcombe offers a complete contrast.

Salcombe is perhaps the ideal place for messing about in boats. A sheltered harbour on an exposed coast and the calm waters of the estuary to explore at high tide – where could be better. The Kingsbridge Estuary is very different from others in South Devon in that there is no major river flowing into it. Instead it has nine small streams, each flowing into its own tributary creek, creating a landscape which is very gentle and very beautiful. Climb the hill above the ferry at East Portlemouth, or walk out on to Snapes Point to appreciate it. As on the Dart, you can see it from a pleasure boat, but here you really need your own dinghy or canoe to explore. Land at Kingsbridge if you can – another interesting and bustling town.

Back at Salcombe take time to wander the waterfront and absorb the magnificent setting of the town before boarding the little ferry which runs down to South Sands, and perhaps being surprised at how you are taken ashore!

Now we come to what must be the most spectacular cliff scenery on this coast – Bolt Head to Bolt Tail. Walk out past the pinnacles at Sharp Tor and enjoy the splendour of it all the way. Be there in Spring or early Summer and the flowers will amaze you – golden gorse, carpets of pink thrift, white sea campion and yellow kidney vetch are an absolute delight. Try to be on Bolt Tail as the sun goes down. It is a dramatic situation, and one of the few places on this coast which faces the right way to get a summer sunset over the sea.

Great Mattiscombe Sand, just west of Start Point.

'Cornish hedges' near Prawle Point.

Elender Cove, below Gammon Head, is idyllic.

Thrift and sparkle.

Late afternoon west of Prawle Point.

The Kingsbridge Estuary just after sunset, from above East Portlemouth.

Salcombe Harbour on a still morning.

52

Mist clearing from Salcombe Harbour.

Salcombe has a fascinating waterfront and a misty morning adds atmosphere. Snape Point, on the other side of Batson Creek, offers wonderful views of the town and up the river on a clear day.

The sun breaking through mist at Salcombe.

56

Kingsbridge is a bustling little town at the head of the estuary.

Flowering gorse gives a wonderful show between Bolt Head and Bolt Tail.

The pinnacles at Sharp Tor.

Rocky ridges near Soar Mill Cove.

Opposite page: *Soar Mill Cove.*

The sun setting over Bigbury Bay, from Bolt Tail.

BIGBURY BAY AND THE RIVER AVON

From Bolt Tail to Burgh Island the coast has a different feel to it. The cliffs are lower and less wild, the beaches are bigger, and despite the fact that Bantham gets the biggest and best surf on this coast, it seems gentle and friendly. It is also more easily accessible by car and is very busy in Summer. You can join the happy throng of surfers, sunbathers, kite-flyers and sandcastle-builders or, if you are willing to walk a little way, you can still find an uncrowded beach. If you want real peace and quiet, leave the beaches behind and explore the wonderful estuary of the River Avon.

Walking from Bolt Tail down into Hope Cove this changed character is immediately apparent. The bay is a favourite summer anchorage for visiting yachts and the little harbour shelters numerous small craft. Thurlestone Rock dominates the view as you follow the coast path round to the beaches of Thurlestone itself, a favourite haunt for windsurfers and scuba divers. A stroll along the edge of the golf course above a rocky foreshore with little sandy coves then brings you to the top of the hill overlooking Bantham.

I could fill a whole book with shots of Bantham – surf rolling in to the great wide beach, the sand dunes of the Ham with their butterflies and orchids, that beautiful curve of the Avon past those picturesque boathouses, and so many people enjoying the place in so many different ways. Even when it is really busy I still love to go there.

Perhaps the best way to arrive is by canoe. Launch by that unexpected little tidal road at Aveton Gifford and float down the river between steep wooded banks. Little egrets, herons, and sometimes kingfishers will let you get very close, and there are plenty of places where you can land for a picnic. Spend some time on the beach at Bantham and paddle back on the flood tide – a superb day out. If you don't have a boat, the signposted Avon Estuary Walk allows you to explore on foot what must be one of the most beautiful waterways in the country, and you can even make a circuit of it by using the (summer only) ferry that plies between Bantham and Cockleridge on the Bigbury side of the river.

Bigbury is another busy place – a favourite for a family day on the beach, and full of interest. At low tide you can walk across the causeway to rocky Burgh Island with its extravagant art deco hotel and cosy Pilchard Inn. On the seaward side of the island there are some dramatic cliffs, covered in pink thrift in the Spring and home to a colony of cormorants. If you linger too long and find yourself cut off by the rising tide, don't worry – you can return on the amazing 'Heath Robinson' sea tractor which carries you high and dry back to the mainland. As you ride, you can look westwards along the wild and little-frequented coast which we are going to explore next.

Descending into Hope Cove from Bolt Tail.

Sunset beyond the church at Hope Cove.

The Long Stone, near Bantham.

One of several sandy bays between Hope Cove and Bantham.

Low tide at Bantham.

The beach at Bantham is a hive of activity in Summer, but there is space to find peace and quiet, especially late in the day.

Evening on the river at Bantham.

Enjoying the evening sun by the slipway at Bantham.

Pyramidal orchids on the Ham.

Jenkin's Quay at the back of the Ham.

One of two beautiful figureheads on the boat-house by the slipway.

Cockleridge Beach on the Bigbury side of the river, from above Jenkin's Quay.

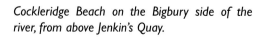

Low tide on the Avon…

...a beautiful sandy estuary

Aveton Gifford at the head of the Avon Estuary.

A little oak wood by the Avon Estuary Walk

High tide at Aveton Gifford…

…with marker posts showing the line of the tidal road.

At low tide there is plenty of space on the beach at Bigbury...

…especially if you walk round towards Cockleridge.

The main beach at Bigbury is a favourite with families, windsurfers and kite-flyers. Cross over to Burgh Island and you will find a more peaceful place with towering cliffs and carpets of thrift on the seaward side.

Sunset over Burgh Island, with the causeway just showing.

BURGH ISLAND TO WONWELL AND THE ERME

From Bigbury we reach Challaborough almost immediately. If you enjoy a good surfing beach, a waterfront pub, and the option of staying in one of the caravans on the big site which runs up the valley behind, you will like it. Beyond here the cliffs are big and wild, and isolated coves which elsewhere would appear friendly and inviting seem here to be part of this wildness – beautiful, but lonely and aloof. At Wonwell the coast turns in to the Erme Estuary which is another unspoiled gem.

The first part of the coast path is a switchback which will test legs, lungs and determination. On very low spring tides it is just possible to scramble along the foreshore to Ayrmer Cove, but I wouldn't recommend it unless you are very sure-footed and certain of the tide times! Likewise, it is sometimes possible to get from there to Westcombe Beach through an impressive rock arch, but unless it is close to low water you will have to climb up and over the cliff on the coast path. Whichever route you arrive by, the effort is worthwhile, for this beach has some of the finest rock architecture to be found in the South Hams. A row of sharp pinnacles runs out to sea, carved from incredibly smooth and shiny rock, eroded into shapes which are almost sensuous in their curves and contortions. Every photographer should come to this beach at least once. From here you have to climb up and over Hoist Point, and follow the cliff-top path looking down on to inaccessible coves and jagged offshore rocks, with an unforgettable view back towards Burgh Island.

At Muxham Point we turn the corner and see the the Erme for the first time, and very impressive it is. If the tide is high and ebbing, and a swell is running, the waves steepen and march up the river for almost half a mile before breaking and dying in a welter of foam – conditions which competent surfers and windsurfers will revel in, but others beware! If the tide is out you will be confronted by a huge expanse of beach with the river meandering across it in shallow channels, and the sand moulded into fantastic ripple patterns by the power of the tides and the waves. You can stroll up the river along the beach for some way at low tide, past the old lime kiln, and a beautiful walk it is. The haunting cry of the curlew and the raucous croak of the heron may be the only sounds you will hear. Sit for a while and just soak up the peacefulness of this place. You will have to return the same way, as the higher reaches of the estuary are lacking in public paths and can only be explored if permission is obtained from the landowner, but perhaps it is this which keeps the place so special.

There is no ferry across the mouth of the Erme, and that seems right for a place which is remote and unspoiled, but for a longish period either side of low water it is possible to wade across safely on a line between the slipways at Wonwell and Mothecombe. It is worth getting wet feet to walk the next section to the west!

On the cliffs above Hoist Beach.

Westcombe Beach — a delightful and uncrowded spot.

Into the light from Westcombe Beach.

The pinnacles at Westcombe Beach.

An impressive stretch of coast looking towards Ayrmer Cove.

The mouth of the Erme – a good surf spot.

Looking up the Erme to Wonwell beach.

Driftwood sculpture at Wonwell.

Ripple patterns demonstrate the power of wave and tide in the mouth of the Erme.

The upper reaches of the Erme are quiet and beautiful.

The old limekiln at Wonwell.

Gentle waves as the sun sets over Wonwell beach.

THE ERME TO THE YEALM AND BEYOND

Again, this is a stretch of coast for the connoisseur. There are few accessible beaches, but some which can be reached without a boat are delightful. The pretty twin villages of Newton Ferrers and Noss Mayo are hidden a little way up the Yealm – another quiet and unspoiled estuary. To the west lies the popular beach of Wembury, from where the coast turns in towards Plymouth.

If you have forded the Erme from Wonwell, walk around the foreshore or over the cliff to Meadowsfoot Beach – a pretty little cove from where the coast path runs high above a rocky shore with occasional delightful beaches. You can scramble down to one or two of them and swim through a maze of narrow sandy-bottomed channels. I recall one day in the blazing hot summer of 2003 when the water at Gull Cove was as warm and crystal-clear as the Mediterranean and it was pure pleasure to just slip into it after a few hot miles of walking the cliffs.

St Anchorite's Rock is the next landmark before we join the old Revelstoke carriage drive to Noss Mayo. This provides an exhilarating and well-graded scenic route for six glorious miles around the cliffs. Stride out and enjoy the long views past the Great Mew Stone down into Cornwall – if visibility is really good you may see as far as the Lizard. But it's not always like that – some years ago my wife and I struggled along here on a day when the wind was gusting to 80mph, literally holding each other up at times. In the fjord-like mouth of the Yealm the waves were really big, and the wind was blowing the tops off them – not as spray, but as great slugs of solid water.

At Mouthstone Point it is well worth dropping down the grassy slope on to the lower path round to Cellar Beach, a favourite lunchtime anchorage for yachts and another good place for a swim. A little way on there is a summer-only ferry across to Warren Point, but don't miss the walk around Newton Creek through Noss Mayo and Newton Ferrers. They and their situation are delightful, and the waterfront pubs are a good enough reason to linger and watch the boats on the river. At the western end of Newton Ferrers the same ferry that we passed earlier on the other shore, also picks up here for Warren Point. But before you make the crossing it is worth walking the mile or so up through Newton Wood, alongside the main channel of the Yealm. From the far end of the wood you will be able to appreciate the charm and beauty of the higher reaches of the estuary.

The walk along the cliff path from Warren Point is dominated by the bold triangular wedge of Great Mew Stone, providing a focal point in that restless expanse of ocean. Try to arrive at Wembury at low tide so that you can explore the rock pools – they really are worth seeing. Beyond here the coast begins to have a slightly suburban feel to it, but do not be deterred – it also has some nice little beaches, some fascinating coastal fortifications from various periods of history, and the constant interest of boats and shipping of all shapes and sizes entering and leaving Plymouth Sound.

Meadowsfoot Beach with its old seawater swimming pool.

An early morning dip at Meadowsfoot Beach.

104

Gull cove – a wonderful swimming spot.

105

St Anchorite's Rock from Blackaterry Point.

Rock Samphire grows just out of reach of the waves.

East from below St Anchorite's Rock, with Burgh Island in the distance.

There are long views into Cornwall from the Revelstoke carriage drive.

A calm anchorage off Cellar Beach, in the mouth of the Yealm.

Noss Mayo church, above Newton Creek.

The little harbour by Ferry Cottage, opposite Warren Point.

Newton Ferrers from Noss Mayo.

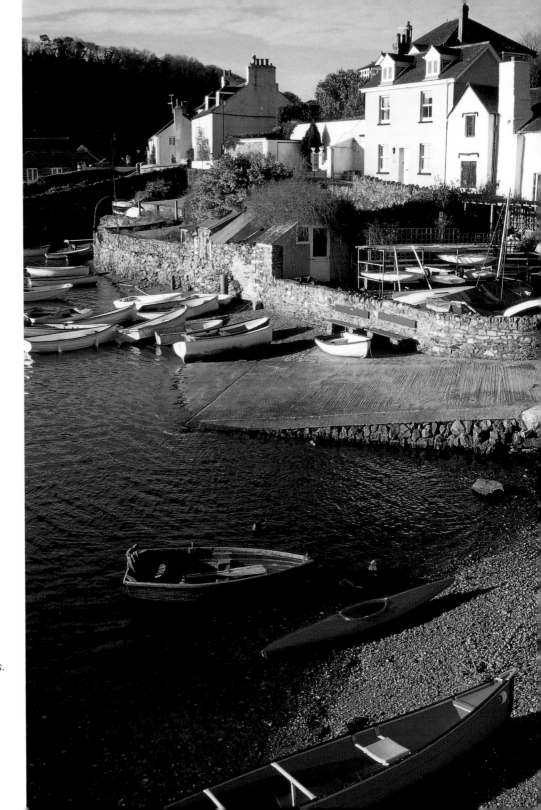

The slipway at Newton Ferrers.

Laid up for the winter on the quay at Bridgend.

Colourful rowing boats on the foreshore.

The middle reaches of the Yealm offer sheltered moorings...

...views of which can be enjoyed from the path up to Newton Wood.

Wembury has interesting rock pools…

... and a wonderfully situated church.

Patterns on an old groyne at Wembury Point.

Waves at Wembury.

Wembury Beach reflecting the sunset.

AWAY FROM THE SEA AND ON TO DARTMOOR

Away from the coast there is green rolling farmland, dotted with villages and dissected by wooded valleys winding up into the remoteness of Dartmoor. Dartmoor is often characterised as the last great wilderness in southern England, but around its moorland core are landscapes which are soft and pretty. Granite tors add a touch of drama; whisky-coloured rivers run clear and fast; ancient woods shelter in the valleys and prehistoric remains add an aura of mystery and timelessness.

The Dart is the biggest river in the area, beloved of fishermen in summer and canoeists in winter. Above Totnes the valley winds through farmland, past Dartington's beautiful mediaeval buildings and peaceful gardens before narrowing and deepening at Buckfast. Beyond here it becomes heavily wooded and progressively more rocky until, upstream of New Bridge, you are into a wild landscape.

The headwaters of the Dart lie on the northern part of Dartmoor, beyond the South Hams, but the other main rivers – the Avon, Erme, Yealm and Plym, all rise on the heights of the south moor. Their upper reaches cross moorland which is remote and empty now but which was clearly a hive of activity in Bronze Age and more recent historical times. Just look at a large-scale Ordnance Survey map to see the number of hut circles, enclosures, cairns, stone rows and other prehistoric sites. Look again and you will find reference to later tin-mining and clay-working, granite quarries, mineral tramways and a host of other fascinating remains which together make up an archaeological landscape second to none. The rivers themselves are delightful, with pretty falls and deep pools, darting trout and dippers. Away from the moor they flow through valleys which are often narrow, steep-sided and wooded, with ancient bridges and occasional towns and villages. They are gentle in Summer but powerful when in flood.

Between the major valleys is rolling farmland, quite high in places, heavily dissected by tributary streams and dotted with farms, hamlets and villages. Not all of the villages are chocolate-box pretty, but they are all interesting, with picturesque cottages, ancient pubs and churches which are both historic and beautiful. The one inland town of any size is Ivybridge, which rather lost its charm in a sea of housing development, but which is now regaining its identity as a thriving and attractive centre serving the surrounding areas. Wherever you go the network of narrow country lanes is a delight to explore, with magnificent displays of wild flowers in Spring and early Summer. This is rural Devon as we all imagine it should be, and well worth discovering when you fancy a change from the more dramatic landscapes of the coast and Dartmoor.

Looking across the Avon valley from Churchstow – rolling countryside rising up to the heights of Dartmoor.

The Erme valley near Holbeton.

Evening light on the upper Dart valley, from Combestone Tor.

A golden glow over Venford Reservoir, on Holne Moor.

The upper Dart is a favourite with canoeists.

Autumn colour in Hembury Woods, by the Dart.

Dartington has wonderful mediaeval buildings and superb gardens.

Looking across the Avon valley from Brent Hill.

The lower Avon runs through quiet woodlands and under ancient bridges.

The upper Erme valley, looking down on Piles Copse.

The path through Piles Copse.

The upper Plym valley from Little Trowles-worthy Tor.

The Dewerstone, with the far side of the Plym valley in deep shadow.

Stalldown stone row, on the watershed between the Erme and the Yealm.

Evidence of abandoned granite working on Trowlesworthy Tors.

Pretty waterfalls at Yealm Steps.

The Erme through the old bridge at Ivybridge.

Ivybridge sits in the Erme valley. The main South West rail line crosses the river on a soaring viaduct, with the piers of the original Brunel structure standing alongside. Victorian Stowford Mill still produces paper.

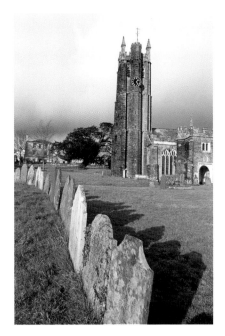

Inland villages in the South Hams are not generally chocolate-box style, but they are well worth visiting, and many have interesting churches. Here we have (top) Harberton with its beautifully restored screen; and the famous crooked spire at Ermington.

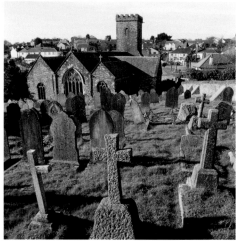

Ashprington church (opposite, top left) is imposing, Slapton nestles under its ruined chantry tower, Ugborough is seen through the church gate and Loddiswell across the cemetery. On this page we have thatched roofs in Thurlestone, colourful cottages at South Brent, and the village street climbing up the hill at Modbury.

South Brent sits under isolated Brent Hill.

Holbeton is tucked into a hollow above the Erme.

I came across this happy couple early one morning, sitting outside the pub in Ermington. Must have been a good night!